MUSIC MAKERS

Guitars

by Cynthia Amoroso and Robert B. Noyed

Pluck, pluck. Strum, strum.
It is time to play the guitar!

Playing the guitar is fun to do.

The guitar is a **string instrument**. Most guitars have six strings. Some guitars have four or even 12 strings. Each string makes a different sound.

Each guitar string has a different thickness.

A person plucks, or strums, a string with his or her hand. This string **vibrates** and makes a sound. These sounds are called notes. The notes can be high or low.

A guitar's sound comes from a plucked string.

People play guitars using their fingers. Some people use a **pick**. Strumming one string at a time makes one note. Strumming more than one string makes a **chord**.

Some players use guitar picks.

There are many kinds of guitars. An **electric guitar** is plugged into an **amplifier**. This makes the guitar louder.

An amplifier makes an electric guitar louder.

Most guitars are made of wood. An **acoustic guitar** has a hole in it. The hole helps make the sound.

An acoustic guitar's hole helps make the sound.

People have played guitars for a long time. **Egyptians** of long ago played instruments like guitars. People all over the world play guitars.

Men in Mexico play guitars in a band.

People make many kinds of music with guitars. Two kinds are folk and rock.

A guitar player must tune the instrument.

Guitars are sometimes played alone. They are played alongside other instruments, too. People often play guitars while someone sings. Many bands have guitars.

A girl plays a guitar at band practice.

Pluck, pluck. Strum, strum. Playing the guitar is fun!

A person can learn to play the guitar at a young age.

Glossary

acoustic guitar (uh-KOO-stik gih-TAR): An acoustic guitar is a guitar that does not need an amplifier. A person can play many kinds of music with an acoustic guitar.

amplifier (AM-pluh-fye-ur): An amplifier is a machine that makes something louder. An electric guitar uses an amplifier.

chord (KORD): A chord is several notes played at once. A chord can be played on a guitar.

Egyptians (ih-JIP-shunz): Egyptians are people who live in the country of Egypt. Egyptians of long ago played a kind of guitar.

electric guitar (ih-LEK-trik gih-TAR): An electric guitar is a guitar that uses an amplifier. A rock band has an electric guitar.

pick (PIK): A pick is a small piece of metal or plastic that is used to pluck guitar strings. A person may play the guitar with a pick.

string instrument (STRING IN-struh-munt): A string instrument is an instrument that makes sound by pressing or plucking strings. The guitar is a string instrument.

vibrates (VY-brayts): Something that moves back and forth very quickly vibrates. When guitar strings vibrate, they make a sound.

To Find Out More

Books

Bay, William. *Children's Guitar Method: Volume 1.* Pacific, MO: Mel Bay Publications, 2003.

Claybourne, Anna. *The Science of a Guitar.* Strongsville, OH: Gareth Stevens, 2009.

Manus, R., and L. C. Hernsberger. *Kid's Guitar Course, Book 1.* Van Nuys, CA: Alfred Music, 2003.

Web Sites

Visit our Web site for links about guitars: *childsworld.com/links*

Note to Parents, Teachers, and Librarians: We routinely verify our Web links to make sure they are safe and active sites. So encourage your readers to check them out!

Index

About the Authors

Cynthia Amoroso has worked as an elementary school teacher and a high school English teacher. Writing children's books is another way for her to share her passion for the written word.

Robert B. Noyed has worked as a newspaper reporter and in the communications department for a Minnesota school district. He enjoys the challenge and accomplishment of writing children's books.

On the cover: Both hands are used to play the guitar.

Published by The Child's World®
1980 Lookout Drive • Mankato, MN 56003-1705
800-599-READ • www.childsworld.com

ACKNOWLEDGMENTS
The Child's World®: Mary Berendes, Publishing Director
The Design Lab: Design and production
Red Line Editorial: Editorial direction

PHOTO CREDITS: iStockphoto, cover, 3, 21; JustASC/Shutterstock, 5; Condor 36/Shutterstock, 7; Michelle Junior/iStockphoto, 9; Big Stock Photo, 11; Richard Thomas/123rf, 13; Travel Bug/Shutterstock, 15; Brian Weed/Shutterstock, 17; Anna Lubovedskaya/iStockphoto, 19

Printed in the United States of America in Mankato, Minnesota.
November 2009
F11460

LIBRARY OF CONGRESS CATALOGING-IN-PUBLICATION DATA
Amoroso, Cynthia.
  Guitars / by Cynthia Amoroso and Robert B. Noyed.
    p. cm. — (Music makers)
  Includes index.
  ISBN 978-1-60253-354-7 (library bound : alk. paper)
  1. Guitar—Juvenile literature. I. Noyed, Robert B. II. Title. III. Series.
  ML1015.G9A45 2010
  787.87'19—dc22   2009030206